12 ENTERTAINERS
WITH DISABILITIES

by Marne Ventura

STORY LIBRARY
MORE TO EXPLORE

FX,9-2∞

www.12StoryLibrary.com

12-Story Library is an imprint of Bookstaves.

Photographs ©: Richard Bailey/sarahgordy.com, cover, 1; Tinseltown/Shutterstock.com, 4; Jac.de Nijs/Anefo/CC1.0, 5; Kathy Hutchins/Shutterstock.com, 6; Kathy Hutchins/Shutterstock.com, 7; Bollywood Hungama/CC3.0, 8; Nadya Peek/CC2.0, 9; Kathy Hutchins/Shutterstock.com, 10; Jordan Strauss/Invision/Associated Press, 11; Featureflash Photo Agency/Shutterstock.com, 12; Peggy und Marco Lachmann-Anke/PD, 13; Ga Fullner/Shutterstock.com, 14; PD, 15; Everett Collection/Shutterstock.com, 15; Wasforgas/CC3.0, 16; Featureflash Photo Agency/Shutterstock.com, 17; Russell G Sneddon/PICWR/Associated Press, 18; PD, 19; TEDxYouth/YouTube, 20; 5 News/YouTube, 21; Mgersh/CC4.0, 22; Rob Mieremet/Anefo/CC1.0, 23; Album/Alamy, 24; Victor Diaz Lamich/CC3.0, 25; SD Mack/Shutterstock.com, 26; Archives du 7e Art/Walt Disney Pictures/Alamy, 27; goodluz/Shutterstock.com, 28; Belish/Shutterstock.com, 29

ISBN
9781632357540 (hardcover)
9781632358639 (paperback)
9781645820383 (ebook)

Library of Congress Control Number: 2019938632

Printed in the United States of America
October 2019

About the Cover
Actress Sarah Gordy in a period costume inspired by Vermeer.

Access free, up-to-date content on this topic plus a full digital version of this book. Scan the QR code on page 31 or use your school's login at 12StoryLibrary.com.

Table of Contents

Stevie Wonder: Child Prodigy

Stevie Wonder in 2016.

Stevie Wonder is an American singer, songwriter, and musician. He was born Steveland Judkins in 1950 in Michigan. Because he was born six weeks early, he was put into an incubator. Too much oxygen caused him to be blind. By age eight, Stevie was an amazing musician. At 11, he signed a contract with Motown Records. The record company owner nicknamed him Little Stevie Wonder. He recorded his first song at 12.

By the time Wonder was 13, he had a US No. 1 hit single and album. He is the youngest person to have achieved this. His "Fingertips, Part 2" was the first live recording to top the charts. By 1964, he was called simply Stevie Wonder. He sang, wrote songs, and played the harmonica, piano, organ, and drums.

Wonder's contract with Motown ended when he was 21. He began producing his own music. Within a few years, Wonder was one of the best-known African American musicians. He is a pioneer in the use of electronic keyboard instruments. His genres include rock, jazz, and black church music.

25

Number of Grammys Stevie Wonder has won

- In 1973, he was the first African American to win Album of the Year.
- He won again in 1974 and 1976.
- In 1989, Wonder became the youngest living artist to be inducted into the Rock and Roll Hall of Fame. He was 38 years old.

Wonder performing in 1967.

AFRICAN AMERICAN ANTHEMS

Some of Wonder's songs became the theme songs for protestors and activists. His 1966 recording of Bob Dylan's "Blowin' in the Wind" was used for the civil rights movement. "Living for the City" (1973) tackled poverty in black inner cities. His 1980 recording of "Happy Birthday" helped make Dr. Martin Luther King Jr.'s birthday a US holiday.

2

Marlee Matlin: Youngest Best Actress

21

Marlee Matlin's age when she won the Best Actress Oscar

- Matlin signed the national anthem at the Super Bowl in 2016.
- She received a star on the Hollywood Walk of Fame in 2009.
- She also won a Golden Globe Best Actress Award in 1987.

Marlee Matlin is an American actress. She was born in Illinois in 1965. An illness caused hearing loss at 18 months. Her parents refused to send her away to a special school. They encouraged her to use her voice. She learned American Sign Language (ASL). She played with the neighborhood kids. She wore hearing aids.

Matlin started her acting career when she was seven. At a performing arts center for children, she won the starring role in *The Wizard of Oz*. In 1985, she acted in a play in Chicago called *Children of a Lesser God*. A film director saw Matlin's performance. She chose Matlin for the lead role in the film version. Matlin plays a hearing-impaired cleaning woman at a school for the deaf. Her performance earned her the Best Actress Academy Award. At the time,

Matlin helps fit a hearing aid at a Starkey Hearing Foundation event.

she was the youngest Oscar winner. She is still the only Oscar winner who is deaf.

Matlin studied criminal justice in college. This helped her get roles in many TV series about the criminal justice system. Matlin continues to act in movies and TV. She has traveled all over the world. When traveling, she visits both hearing children and those who are hearing impaired.

AMERICAN SIGN LANGUAGE

Marlee Matlin and many other people who are deaf use ASL. This is a visual language of hand movements, facial expressions, and body movements. Historians aren't sure how it began. It has been around for more than 200 years. There are hand positions for the letters of the alphabet. There are movements for common words and phrases.

Sudha Chandran: Determined to Dance

Sudha Chandran in 2012.

didn't clean her cuts properly. They became infected. Chandran's leg had to be amputated.

Chandran specialized in a type of classical Indian dance. It is very old and very demanding. Dancers dress in colorful costumes. They bend their legs in deep squats. Their feet beat in complex rhythms. They move their arms, necks, and shoulders in specific ways. They tell stories with hand and eye movements.

Sudha Chandran is an Indian dancer. Born in 1965, she began dance lessons when she was three. At 17, she hurt her right leg in a bus accident. It wasn't a bad injury, but many other people were also hurt.

In the confusion, the doctors

Chandran loved dancing. She didn't want to give it up. She got a rubber prosthetic leg. After two years of work, she was able to perform as a dancer again. She starred in a film that was based on her life story. It won 14 awards. Chandran is also a TV star in India. She is a judge on two reality dance contest shows.

30
Number of films Sudha Chandran has starred in

- Chandran has a master's degree in economics.
- Her life story is part of the curriculum for school children in India.
- She won the 1986 Special Jury Award at India's National Film Awards.

JAIPUR FOOT

Sudha Chandran was able to dance after her accident. She used a prosthetic called a Jaipur Foot. A team of doctors in India provides artificial limbs for free to people in need. The group has helped 1.55 million amputees in India and 27 other countries across the world.

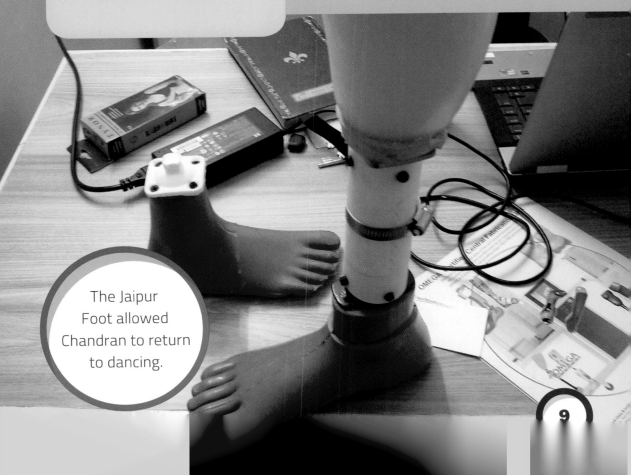

The Jaipur Foot allowed Chandran to return to dancing.

RJ Mitte: Award-Winning Actor

RJ Mitte in 2019.

built up enough strength to stop wearing braces.

Mitte and his family moved to Los Angeles in 2006. Mitte began training to be an actor. He auditioned for TV ads and shows. He became a regular on *Hannah Montana*. In 2008, Mitte was cast as the son of the main character on

5
Number of times RJ Mitte auditioned for the role of Walter Jr. in *Breaking Bad*

- Mitte uses crutches in his part on *Breaking Bad* but doesn't need them in real life.
- He was 14 years old when he started acting.
- He finished high school by mail while he was working as an actor.

RJ Mitte is an American actor. Born in Louisiana in 1992, he has mild cerebral palsy (CP) caused by not getting enough oxygen at birth. CP affects Mitte's muscle control. As a child, he wore leg braces. He loved football. But his coordination made it too difficult to play. He switched to soccer and

Mitte attends The Power of TV: Representing Disability in Storytelling with fellow actors in 2019.

Breaking Bad. His character has more severe CP than Mitte, so he had to learn to walk on crutches. He had to slow down his speech for the part.

The *Breaking Bad* series was named Best Drama at the 2013 and 2014 Golden Globe Awards. It won the 2012, 2013, and 2014 Screen Actors Guild (SAG) awards for Best Ensemble. Mitte won Best Performance in a TV Series by a Young Actor in 2013. *Breaking Bad* won 148 awards in all.

The success of *Breaking Bad* made Mitte a celebrity. He was a model for the clothing maker Gap. He went on to star in the series *Switched at Birth*. He has also become a spokesperson for people with disabilities. He is an ambassador for United Cerebral Palsy and Shriners Hospitals for Children.

Michael J. Fox: Actor and Activist

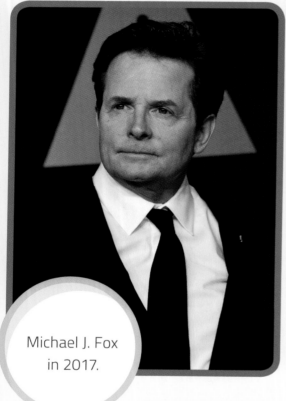

Michael J. Fox in 2017.

Michael J. Fox is an American actor. Born in Alberta, Canada, in 1961, he grew up on Army bases. He began acting when he was a teenager. His first role was in a Canadian sitcom when he was 15. He moved to Los Angeles to pursue a career in acting when he was 18.

In 1982, he was cast as Alex on the TV series *Family Ties*. The series ran for seven years. Fox became one of the best-known young actors in the United States. He also starred in several films, including the three *Back to the Future* movies.

In 1991, Fox found out he has Parkinson's. This is a nerve disease. It causes loss of muscle control. Fox didn't tell the public about his condition for seven years. In 1999, he became an American citizen. In 2000, he retired from the sitcom *Sin City*. He started a foundation to fund research for a cure.

In 2012, Fox returned to acting. From 2013–2014, he starred in his own sitcom, playing a news anchor with Parkinson's. He continues to act in TV series.

A scene from *Back to the Future*.

2002

Year when Michael J. Fox received a star on the Hollywood Walk of Fame

- Fox has won five Emmys and four Golden Globe awards.
- He has written three books about his life.
- He is a spokesperson for Parkinson's, bringing hope and humor to his condition.

BACK TO THE FUTURE

In Fox's role as Marty McFly, he plays a teenager in a small California town. His mad scientist friend invents a time machine-sports car, and McFly travels back in time. Fox was 24 years old when he made *Back to the Future*. He was also starring in *Family Ties*, so he worked 16 hours a day.

Daniel Radcliffe: Boy Wizard

Daniel Radcliffe in 2013.

Radcliffe is best known for playing Harry Potter, the orphan boy who finds out he is a wizard. He starred in the leading role of *Harry Potter and the Sorcerer's Stone* in 2001. The film was a big success. Radcliffe continued to star in the following seven Harry Potter films. The last was made in 2011. Radcliffe had roles in nine more films between 2007 and 2017. He also starred in a

Daniel Radcliffe is an English actor. Born in London in 1989, he began his acting career as a monkey in a school play at age six. In 1999, he was cast as the character David Copperfield in a British TV series. In 2001, he had a part in a spy movie.

Between 6 and 10 percent
Number of children who show signs of dyspraxia

- Radcliffe has 15 wins and 43 nominations for acting awards.
- His star was added to the Hollywood Walk of Fame in 2015.
- His success story is an inspiration to young people.

Radcliffe in 2001 when he starred in *Harry Potter and the Sorcerer's Stone*.

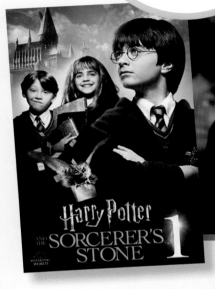

THINK ABOUT IT

Daniel Radcliffe raises awareness about dyspraxia. How do you think his success as an actor affects other people with disabilities?

TV series and seven theater productions.

Radcliffe has dyspraxia. This disorder can cause poor balance and coordination, vision problems, difficulty reading, and poor social skills. For Radcliffe, dyspraxia makes it hard for him to write by hand and tie shoelaces. He found school challenging and felt he wasn't good at anything.

After becoming a celebrity for his role as Harry Potter, Radcliffe has helped to raise awareness about dyspraxia. He advises young people not to let a learning disability hold them back. He points out that some of the smartest people he knows have learning disabilities.

15

Susan Boyle: She's Got Talent

Susan Boyle is a Scottish singer. She was born in Blackburn, West Lothian, in 1961. For years, doctors said she had brain damage. She had problems in school. Other children teased her. But she loved to sing. At age 12, she was in her first musical. After high school, she studied acting. She also sang in the church choir and at local music festivals.

In 1995, Boyle tried out for a British TV talent show. She was not chosen, but she kept trying to become a professional singer. She recorded a song for a local charity. She recorded and mailed a demo CD to record companies, radio stations, TV shows, and talent contests. She took more voice lessons and recorded more demos. In 2008, she tried out for *Britain's Got Talent*. She earned a chance to sing on the show. Her performance in 2009 was

Susan Boyle performs in 2013.

a great success. The entire audience stood up and clapped. The video went viral.

In 2009, Boyle recorded her first studio album. It included the song from *Britain's Got Talent*. The song hit No. 1 and the album sold more than 3 million copies. It was the second-best-selling album of the year.

100 million

Estimated number of people worldwide who have seen Boyle's video

- Boyle won second place on the show.
- She had been trying for success as a singer for many years.
- She didn't find out she has Asperger's until she was 52 years old.

Boyle at the Pride of Britain Awards in 2012.

Boyle always felt doctors were wrong when they said she had brain damage. In 2012, she asked a specialist to recheck her condition. He said she has Asperger's syndrome. This causes Boyle to have trouble in social settings. She has mood swings. But her intelligence is above average.

Francesca Martinez: Wobbly Comedian

Francesca Martinez in 2014.

Francesca Martinez is an English comedian. She was born in London in 1978. Her father was Spanish, and her mother was Swedish and English. When she was two years old, doctors told her parents she had cerebral palsy (CP). The doctors also said she was mentally retarded. Martinez's parents disagreed. They didn't make a big deal about her CP. They gave her lots of love and support.

When Martinez started elementary school, she wasn't even aware she was different. But by the time she got to high school, she understood that other kids saw her as abnormal. She began to try to hide her CP. It caused her to shake and wobble. It was so difficult to control that she stopped going out in public when she didn't have to.

At age 14, Martinez landed a part on a British TV series for teenagers. After five years of success on the show, she still felt bad about her condition. In 1999, she joined a comedy group. For her routine, she stood on stage and talked about her condition. She joked about her wobbliness. She was honest about who she was. It made her feel good about herself. She decided that she wasn't abnormal. She embraced being wobbly.

THINK ABOUT IT

In her book, Francesca Martinez questions the idea that some people are normal and others are not. What does she mean? Do you agree?

2003

Year when Francesca Martinez was named one of the funniest acts in British comedy

- Martinez performs at comedy festivals around the world.
- She published a book about her life in 2014.
- She helps people with disabilities embrace their differences.

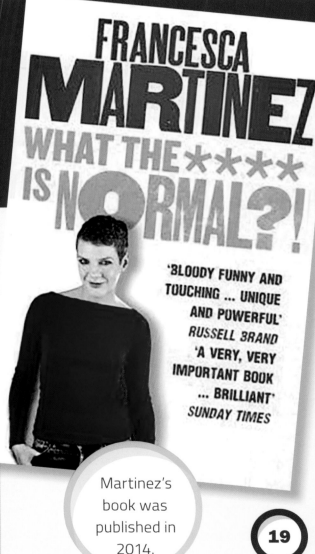

FRANCESCA MARTINEZ
WHAT THE **** IS NORMAL?!

'BLOODY FUNNY AND TOUCHING ... UNIQUE AND POWERFUL'
RUSSELL BRAND
'A VERY, VERY IMPORTANT BOOK ... BRILLIANT'
SUNDAY TIMES

Martinez's book was published in 2014.

Sarah Gordy: Outstanding Achiever

9

British actress Sarah Gordy was born in London in 1978. She has Down syndrome. This condition causes slower than usual mental and physical growth.

As a child, Gordy danced and sang for her family. In elementary school and high school, she acted in plays. After high school, she joined a group of actors with Down syndrome. Next, she joined an arts group for people with disabilities. Gordy landed a role on *Upstairs Downstairs*, a popular, long-running British TV series.

Upstairs Downstairs takes place in the 1930s. Gordy plays a young woman with Down syndrome. She prepared at length for her part. She did workouts to stay in shape. She signed up for a healthy eating program. She spent hours researching what life was like for her character in 1936. She read her lines over and over again.

Next, Gordy was cast in an

Sarah Gordy in 2013 giving a TEDxYouth talk about escaping labels and being different.

episode of *Call the Midwife*, another popular British TV series. She has appeared in many other TV roles and 13 plays. She appeared in three films and six commercials. She has been a model and a member of a dance group. She is an ambassador for a British charity for people with disabilities.

Gordy receives her MBE from Prince William in 2018.

2018

Year when Sarah Gordy became the first woman with Down syndrome to be made an MBE

- MBE stands for Member of the Most Excellent Order of the British Empire.
- The prestigious award is for outstanding achievement or service to the community.
- Prince William gave Gordy her award in person.

THINK ABOUT IT

Sarah Gordy has landed many parts where she plays a person with Down syndrome. She made history by playing a character without a disability at a British theater in 2014. Why was this so important?

José Feliciano: Self-Taught Musician

José Feliciano in 2010.

is like a small accordion. He played music for his classmates in school. When he was nine, he performed at a theater in the Bronx. He taught himself to play guitar by listening to records. Sometimes he practiced for 14 hours a day.

When he was 17, Feliciano quit school. He wanted to help his family by earning money. He began playing guitar and singing in coffeehouses for tips. He would set out a hat or a jar and people would put money in if they liked his music. Critics wrote positive reviews of his performance. An executive from a big record company heard him and gave him a recording contract.

José Feliciano is an American musician. Born blind in 1945 in Puerto Rico, he was one of 11 boys. At age three, he played a tin can drum. His family moved to New York City when he was five. By age six, he had taught himself to play a concertina, which

In 1966, Feliciano began recording Spanish songs. He performed them in a new way that combined Latin rhythms with jazz and rock. His versions were hits. Feliciano became popular with teenagers in Central and South America. In the United

Feliciano performs in Amsterdam in 1970.

1987
Year when José Feliciano was given a star on the Hollywood Walk of Fame

- Feliciano is known for singing his own version of the US National Anthem at the 1968 World Series.
- He has recorded nearly 70 albums.
- He has won seven Grammy awards.

States, he recorded a song called "Light My Fire" that was also a hit. By age 23, Feliciano had won two Grammys for his music. He did some acting in TV series but decided he preferred music.

Ray Charles: Musical Genius

Ray Charles was an American musician. He was born Ray Charles Robinson in 1930 in Georgia. He grew up in Florida. When he was only five years old, he played piano at a local café. He started to lose his eyesight when he was six. The probable cause was an eye disease. By age seven, he was blind. Charles studied music at a school for children who were deaf and blind. His father died when he was 10. His mother died when he was 15.

Charles left school after his mother's death. He worked in dance bands around the state. He dropped his last name so he wouldn't be confused with the popular boxer Sugar Ray Robinson. In 1947, he moved to Seattle. He played blues, jazz, and boogie-woogie piano. He sang with emotion. In 1952, Charles signed a contract with a major record company. In 1959, his song "What'd I Say" was a million-seller.

Charles toured the United States with his band and backup singers, the Raelettes. He made appearances on TV and in films. He did arrangements for other musicians. Charles was a pioneer of soul music. His style combined gospel, rhythm and blues, and jazz. Other musicians called him The Genius.

Ray Charles in 1955.

NOT STOPPED BY BLINDNESS

Charles rode a bike, played chess, used stairs, and even flew an airplane. He felt that hearing loss was a much more tragic disability than blindness. In 1986, he started a foundation to help people with hearing impairment.

13
Number of Grammy awards Ray Charles won

- Charles was inducted into the Rock and Roll Hall of Fame in 1986.
- *Ray*, a movie about his life, came out in 2004.
- He received the Grammy Lifetime Achievement Award in 1987.

Charles performing in 2003, one of the last performances before his death in 2004.

Keira Knightley: Successful Actress

Keira Knightley is a British actress. She was born in 1985 in England. Her father was an actor and her mother was a playwright. Knightly wanted to act from an early age. Because she has dyslexia, it was difficult for her to learn to read. When she was six, she asked her parents to hire an agent for her. Instead, they made a deal. If she would learn to read, they would get her an agent. Knightley studied all summer by reading a screenplay. Her parents hired an agent, and Knightly started her career in acting.

When she was 13, she had a part in a *Star Wars* film. At 17, she starred in the film *Pirates of the Caribbean*. She was nominated for an Oscar for her role in the film *Pride and Prejudice* when she was 20. She was nominated again at age 30 for her role in the film *The Imitation Game*.

DYSLEXIA

Knightley has found many ways to cope with her dyslexia. She says she will always have trouble reading. Some days are easier than others It helps to read out loud. While she's on a movie set, she doesn't chat with others between scenes. It breaks the concentration she needs to act as her character. She also dislikes being recognized as a star strangers. She prefers to be left alone.

28

Number of awards Keira Knightley has won for acting

- Knightley is the only non-American on the highest-paid actress list.
- She starred in her first TV role when she was seven.
- She never had formal training as an actor.

Knightley in *Pirates of the Caribbean.*

Learn More:
Service Animals

Animals have been helping people for thousands of years. Service animals, especially dogs, can be trained to do tasks that people with disabilities can't do on their own. Service animals enable people with disabilities to live fuller, more independent lives.

Guide dogs help people with impaired vision. German shepherds, Labrador retrievers, and golden retrievers are usually chosen. These breeds tend to be calm, smart, helpful, and healthy. Puppies live for a year in a foster home. Next, they get three to five months of special training. They learn to wear a harness, stop at street corners, and help keep their human from bumping into things.

Hearing dogs alert people with hearing impairments to sounds. Mixed-breed dogs rescued from animal shelters usually become hearing dogs. They touch their human with a paw to tell them if their baby is crying or the doorbell is ringing. They lead them to safety if need be.

Mobility dogs help people in wheelchairs. They use a button to open an automatic door. They pick up something their human has dropped. They bring their human a ringing phone. They can wear a harness and pull a wheelchair up a ramp.

Glossary

agent
A person who helps an entertainer get work.

amputate
To cut off.

arrangement
Changes made by a musician or composer to a piece of music.

celebrity
A person who is famous.

contract
A legal agreement between people.

demo
Short for demonstration. A sample of an artist's work.

genre
A type or style of music, art, or literature.

impair
To damage or cause harm to.

incubator
A warm container for babies who are born too early.

prosthesis
A human-made device such as an arm or a leg.

screenplay
A story written for use in a film.

sitcom
Short for situation comedy. A TV show genre.

viral
Quickly spread and popular on the Internet.

Read More

Gigliotti, Jim. *Who is Stevie Wonder?* Who Was? New York: Grosset & Dunlap, 2016.

Hayes, Amy. *Disability Rights Movement.* Civic Participation: Working for Civil Rights. New York: Powerkids Press, 2017.

Yasuda, Anita. *Life with Blindness.* Everyday Heroes. Mankato, MN: Childs World, 2018.

Index

About the Author

Marne Ventura has written over 100 books for children. A former elementary school teacher, she holds a master's degree in education from the University of California. Marne and her husband live on the central coast of California.